Finding Temperance

Mikayla Vittallo

BookLeaf Publishing

Presentation by *BookLeaf Publishing*

Web: www.bookleafpub.com

E-mail: info@bookleafpub.com

ISBN: 9789357214513

First edition 2023

To those that have encouraged me to write.

To those that struggle in their own ways,

but keep seeing the next sunrise.

ACKNOWLEDGEMENT

I want to say thank you to everyone who is reading this, without you this dream from childhood wouldn't exist.

Thank you, to those that sat here helping to ease the anxiety and self-doubt, without you I would be too much mashed potatoes to write.

Thank you, to my sister who protected me in your own way, without you I would have had a harder and longer journey.

Thank you, to my sister who was one of the first people to encourage me to write and help form that childhood dream, without you the passion for writing stories may not have been this strong.

PREFACE

These poems deal with trauma in multiple forms, please take caution while reading.

Morning

exploring,
adventure
this was the idea
of my youth.
a trip into the forest,
to have tea parties with fairies,
to swim with dryads,
to be amongst friends

Expectations

i thought if i became the image that you wanted
you would love me.
If i was better, smarter,
would i ever be enough,
Would I ever be what you wanted?
All i ever wanted was for you to be proud,
for you to say:
"i love you,
my daughter."

But that was never to happen
and now
while i struggle
to figure out how
i am learning to be
proud and love
my own
damn
self.

Storm

my thoughts are crushing in on me
holding my breath as if a taunt,
I can feel their hands,
touching me.
the urge to scream, but there is nothing
No whimper
No noise.
i am pushed back into the waves,
as that night replays.

hoping that there's a morning,
that could end this nightmare.

Lighthouse

i thought i wasn't worth the
time on earth.
folding myself in
to take up less space,
as if that would make my existence
reasonable.
now,
trying to accept that there's value
in just being alive.
in forgiving the person in the mirror,
for the years
of self-hatred.
telling myself that i am worthy
to just live.

Protest

He puts his hands on her
ugly compliments spill out,
i used to sit and watch,
unsure
trembling.
Now i will bite that hand if it
would dare come near me.
I do not hold my tongue,
and smile prettily
like they tell me too.
pushing away while standing my ground
You will not see
the old me.

Escapist

i want to run away,
problems are for a different day.
i know i should face them
just not right
now.
let me collect my thoughts
and be comfortable in myself.
learn to be at peace in this skin.
home in this body.
love in this voice.
i need to not want to run
away from being me.

Shark

i lay sleeping
where the world is safe
my mind can finally rest.
ice crawls up my back
as your fingers trail
over my body.
i want to scream,
and fight.
i want to run

I am freezing from the inside
from where you have touched me.
I am frozen.
Frozen.

Voyage

you see adventure
little wanderer,
but unsure of what
sights to run off to.
but look inside, you
have a calling that
screams out.
there are places that are
yours to travel.
yours to explore.

Run to them.

Witch

there was a time
where I didn't know this pain,
or shame,
where i thought i could be strong
in the face of adversaries.
yet when you reached
down My throat,
and ripped the air out of my lungs,
my heart stopped.
and there was nothing i could do,
for months.

i wish i could ease the sweet air
back into my younger self.
to hold her hand,
and watch what you deserve.
see your world crumble down,
just as You ruined mine.

Wings

There was a friend who said i was
fearless.
because i held spiders,
relentlessly climbing higher,
going into dark rooms blind.

how could i tell her that
i am scared,
i have lived by my terrors
seeking approval to fit in,
pleasing others so they don't leave.
I have never not been afraid.

Flower

i live behind mirrors
hiding behind veils
to never see myself correctly.
and while i am
working towards a
happier life,
part of me longs for this
sadness,
that i've known for so long.
i feel as if i am two parts
of two widely different things
waging a war inside my mind,
to find peace inside myself.

Universe

Every night i watch the stars,
wishing to find somewhere,
to go home.
my soul aches
for a place that i have not been
nor will i ever see.
my heart exists out there among other planets
my senses crave the sensations
from the other stars.
Maybe that's why i long for the moon,
yearning to be somewhere new.

Mirror

"your body is a temple"
yet, all i've been taught
is to hate it,
to have shame for how it looks.
i have no control in that i wish,
to be the image of myself that
i actually like.
but when i try, there's shame in that.
there's shame in everything
a woman does to love herself.

i build this temple,
in the way i desire,
until i am able to stand proud
"this is mine and i love it,
exactly as is."

Sundress

i have always craved travel.
the desire had clawed it's way
into my thoughts, making a nest so deep inside
i could never escape.
always day-dreaming of far off lands.
And finally i took the leap
i traveled, on my own, for myself,
with only my desires to guide me.
And what a wondrous moment i had
experienced.
there was freedom in this rarity,
that i had never known.

Grey

it's okay to be sad,
things are over.
respect yourself to feel
these emotions that
swell like the ocean wave.
but understand your
journey is far from over,
it is twisting,
shifting currents.
maybe for now your
journey is with the river
and not the sea.

Bitch-Fire

you think that i'm mean?
Now that i have the strength
to yell back.
to stand proud,
to not bend to your wants?
That's what makes me a bitch?

Alright.

Call me what you must.
But i will never light myself
on fire for your comfort,
Again.

Villain

there are different stories
that everyone has.
and while there is
a person so Evil
in my mind
that i can't even see his name,
i want to believe that
he was,
is,
or at least will be
good.

Raindrops

New people, new beginnings
changing yourself over
and
Over
until you find a version that you like.
others can change,
just the same.
One who was a villain,
can become an
ally.

Gold

my dear,
i wish you could love yourself
as wholly and warmly
as you love others.
you would see that there
is no cure that you need,
from others, that jeer behind the mask
that they wear,
while you brave face, show nothing
but who you are
and it is beautiful.

Garden

a tiny seed,
that's all you have
sitting, waiting.
the one you leave in the corner, forgotten
the next time you see it,
that seed has grown just a little bit,
with surprise you move the seed
to a more carefully picked spot.
nurturing the seed to grow more,
and with it,
so does your hope.

Homeward

there is Someone
special.
We meet tonight,
the moonlight glowing
as we walk together in peace.
dinner is quiet
as we enjoy the silence.
and after the night is done
there is more to do,
off comes the carefully picked dress,
most likely to catch their interest.
face washed clean,
pjs are put one as we climb into bed
I fall asleep with happiness
and nothing else.